A Conversation with
George Bush

A Conversation with
George
Bush

Held on October 19, 1979
at the American Enterprise Institute for Public Policy Research
Washington, D.C.

Library of Congress Cataloging in Publication Data

Main entry under title:
A Conversation with George Bush.
   (AEI studies ; 271)
      1. United States—Politics and government—
1977–   —Addresses, essays, lectures.
2. United States—Economic policy—1971–
—Addresses, essays, lectures.   3. United States—
Foreign relations—1977–   —Addresses, essays,
lectures.   I. Bush, George, 1924–
II. American Enterprise Institute for Public
Policy Research.   III. Series: American Enterprise
Institute for Public Policy Research AEI studies ;
271.
E872.C68   973.926   80-10725
ISBN 0-8447-3374-1

AEI Studies 271

Preface

This discussion is another in a series of "Conversations" sponsored by AEI with outstanding public figures—in and out of government—and with scholars and specialists who have made noteworthy contributions to the formation of public policy. Since the series was launched in 1975, we have invited to AEI, among others, Senator Richard G. Lugar and Senator Daniel Patrick Moynihan, Lane Kirkland of the AFL-CIO, Secretary of Labor Ray Marshall, Robert Strauss, Gerald Ford, the Reverend Jesse Jackson, Philip Crane, John Connally, and Mayor Marion Barry of Washington, D.C. The format for these conversations —a brief presentation, followed by discussion with members of a limited audience of AEI scholars and guests—is intended to produce a minimum of "talking at" the audience and a maximum of speaking to, and listening to, each other.

This booklet is a transcript of an AEI "Conversation," edited, as lightly as possible, to preserve the informal conversational nature of the discussion. We believe that this sort of exchange offers a perspective on the thinking of important public figures very different from that found in their prepared speeches and published writings. And, we believe, it is an excellent way to encourage the "competition of ideas" that is AEI's trademark.

WILLIAM J. BAROODY, JR.
President
American Enterprise Institute
for Public Policy Research

Introductory Remarks

ROBERT A. GOLDWIN
AEI Resident Scholar

George Bush has had an extraordinary career, extraordinarily successful and extraordinarily varied. He was the youngest United States
Navy carrier pilot in World War II and was highly decorated, either
in spite of or because of being shot down in combat.

He finished Yale University in just two and one-half years, with
a Phi Beta Kappa in economics, and was president of his class and cap-
tain of the baseball team.

He then went to Texas and, within eight years, had cofounded
three successful oil firms, pioneering in offshore oil drilling techniques.

In 1966, he ran for Congress as a Republican from a Democratic
district and not only won that first election, but was reelected without
opposition.

After a political setback in 1970, in the next six years, he served
as the U.S. Ambassador to the United Nations, Republican National
Committee Chairman, Chief of the U.S. Liaison Office in China, and
director of the Central Intelligence Agency (CIA).

Then he faced a real dilemma. What can a fifty-five-year-old successful former pilot, scholar, athlete, businessman, legislator, diplomat,
politician, and intelligence chief do for an encore? What is left that is
a real step up?

The choice is narrow: he could either join AEI full time as a
distinguished fellow or run for president of the United States.
[Laughter.]

George Bush has made his decision, and he appears before us
today to suffer, or enjoy, the consequences.

We call these gatherings "conversations," with a literal intent,
and we ask the audience not to think of themselves as passive listeners.

After his brief presentation, Mr. Bush will join actively in a conversation with the audience. We want more than just a question and answer session. We want arguing, probing, discussing, analyzing, agreeing, and disagreeing. We hope that this conversation will provide a true exchange, real give and take: the ultimate aim is inquiry.

The American Enterprise Institute is a nonprofit, nonpartisan, educational and research organization devoted to improving the quality of discourse and deliberation on matters of public policy.

Although most of those who speak or write under auspices provided by AEI take positions and express partisan views, when they do so they speak for themselves and not for AEI. AEI itself, as an institution, takes no position on public policy issues.

Ambassador Bush, the floor is yours.

A Conversation with
George Bush

Thank you, Bob. Let me begin by making a few observations. I come here troubled about what I see ahead for us in 1981–1982. Things are tough right now, and there is no "quick fix" to make things easy in 1980, but I see special difficulty for this country in 1981 and 1982.

Clearly, the three areas of trouble are inflation, energy, and what I call the diminution of U.S. credibility and respect around the world. That gets into the strategic balance, the conventional force imbalance, and the way other countries perceive the United States.

First I want to say that I am fundamentally optimistic about this country. The fascinating experience of having lived in China reinforces my conviction that ours is a good country, an honorable country, a decent country. We have gone through a self-agony in the 1970s during which we have looked inward; we have apologized for ourselves. We accepted a revisionistic view of our own purpose in Southeast Asia. We seem to be uncertain whether we can cope with and solve problems. We have departed from the fundamentals of economics; we have a Congress that seems to be less than responsive to the current mood of the people; our young people have been turned off by Vietnam and Watergate and by the overpromise and the failure to produce of this administration.

I think it is fair to say that there is concern here. But living in China and behind an Iron Curtain has reinforced my convictions about my own country. My convictions did not really need a lot of reinforcing because I am, in a sense, a traditionalist: I believe that the United States has always been sound of purpose and that we have always wanted to help others. I think we have a fantastic record, but we seem to have lost sight of it.

As we go into the early 1980s, there is no easy answer to the problems that will soon be coming together. Inflation is tough, the problem of energy is extraordinarily difficult, and the problem of credibility in foreign affairs, or the strength of the United States, or the intention of the Soviet Union—these things are very troubling.

In talking to the country, I think we must not over-promise, not pledge a quick and easy solution to enormously difficult problems that have plagued our country here and abroad for a long, long time. Frankly, I think the mood of the American people is one of skepticism about overpromise, and I think we have to recognize that the strength of the system is undermined by that kind of rhetoric, even by its use in the heat of a campaign.

I have had the privilege of meeting individually with some people in this room and with members of groups on some of these problems, and I am convinced there are answers, but there are no easy answers. On the economic side, the answer is to return to the fundamentals. We have failed to try the fundamentals on economics. We went through a period when Keynesian economics was considered the way to solve problems. We never really tried the second half of the Keynesian formula. The first half of the formula required stimulating the economy by excessive or excess government spending. The second half, which we never tried, stipulates that when a government gins up the economy, then it lives not in balance but in surplus. We never tested the second half of the formula, but I do not believe that that general formula is the right approach anyway. The result is that we have had deficits in seventeen of the last eighteen years.

Arthur Burns recently gave a brilliant speech in Belgrade in which he talked about the shift away from sensible economics, and the gradual growth of expectations on the part of the American people that the government would fine-tune the economy and solve all these problems. There is a lot of wisdom in that speech.

As I see the problems, the answers are in returning economics to the fundamentals. I proposed a program at the National Press Club which may not be particularly new, but if all the ingredients were applied, I am convinced the program would brake back the inflationary spiral that is crippling every worker and every saver in this country.

One part of my program calls for limiting the growth of federal spending. I know that is a very common thing to talk about. It has been Republican rhetoric for a long time. But if we are candid with each other, we will admit that it has never been tried. There is no

4

magic number, but I feel the growth of spending should be kept in the range of about 6.8 percent.[1]

If that is accompanied by a cutback on the excesses of regulation, investment and productivity will be stimulated. We have failed to realize that we have simply regulated this country to death, and I believe we now need a letting up. We will need some recision, we will need interpretive relief, we will need people in these regulatory positions who will bring a certain balance to their job and not always approach it from what I see as the extreme on the regulatory spectrum. None of this has been tried. Only recently have we recognized that we have gone too far.

The regulation cutback should be coupled with a supply-side tax cut of $20 billion, to be enacted, if one could wave a wand over the situation, in January 1980. The cut should be divided equally between individuals and business. I think then the economy would be in shape to let the new president put forward a balanced budget in fiscal year 1982.

The supply-side tax cut should emphasize things like homes, down payments on homes. The approach to saving and investment would be similar to that of the Keogh or IRA (Individual Retirement Account) plans.

On the business side, the approach would be to review useful life for depreciation and to provide tax credits on certain kinds of equipment, job credits, and investment credits to help people locate where the unemployed are. The whole utilization of this cut would be not the popular political, across-the-board approach that many feel is the answer, but it would stimulate investment and thus increase productivity and employment in the private sector.

I think it is a good program, and that it offers a sensible answer. I am convinced it would work. When the president put forward a balanced budget in 1982, if that were coupled with an indexation of the tax system, then Congress would be compelled to live within those constraints or to raise taxes. A case could be made that some of the business cuts could be deferred, making them smaller in the earlier years and then larger in the later years; that permits planning to take place and minimizes the risk of exacerbating short-term deficit problems.

---

[1] "The key point Mr. Bush stresses here is maintaining a level of growth significantly less than the rate of inflation—which at the time of these remarks, October 19, 1979, was predicted to be in the 8 to 10 percent range." (Added at the request of an aide to George Bush, during editorial review of this transcript, January 25, 1980.)

There was an interesting and lively economic debate last year on the so-called Kemp-Roth proposal. I did not endorse that proposal at that time, though I was asked to by the chairman of our party, because in my view, a straight across-the-board tax cut, not coupled with spending constraints, would risk exacerbating short-term deficit problems. I felt that way because I did not think investors would have any confidence in that proposal, and investor confidence is essential for a supply-side tax cut to work. If taxes were simply cut across-the-board and demand stimulated in that way, public confidence would suffer. I was afraid that approach would not encourage investment. The approach I have put forward here today seems to me more sensible.

The principal problem today is the economy—inflation. It is on everybody's mind in every part of this country.

Coupled with it, of course, is the question of energy. There is no quick fix for the energy problem, but my belief has been that long-run or short-run artificial constraint of the price of a product guarantees shortage. So I have favored decontrol, and I want it now.

I might say I am a little defensive on this subject of decontrol because I know something about energy, having been in oil-related businesses. That is probably not the best identification for a candidate for public office. But I have never subscribed to the Washington theory that someone who has studied Russian ought to be immediately sent to France, or someone who has studied Chinese ought to be put in Nicaragua. Someone who knows something about energy ought to be in government where something can be done about energy. I feel strongly about this point, and I plead guilty; I do know something about the oil business.

Lest I appear defensive—and I am—I totally sold out of the oil business in 1966. I have no conflict of interest. Anyone who can stand to be bored can look at my tax returns at the FEC (Federal Election Commission), because I put them on record there.

I do believe decontrol is the answer, and that it should be coupled with a windfall profits tax. That may seem inconsistent for someone who fundamentally believes in a market economy, but when the price is driven, at least partially, by a cartel, free market forces do not operate. So I have favored a windfall profits tax coupled with a plow-back provision, which means that corporations, to avoid that higher tax, must put more money into the ground, into alternative sources, into synthetics, into research, into something other than diversification, something that will affect the supply side, or even engineering for the conservation side, of energy.

6

I believe that the combination of a windfall profits tax, decontrol, and plow-back is the right mix to move the United States ahead. I realize that is extraordinarily difficult today, given the makeup of the Congress and the low esteem in which the public holds the oil companies. But I like to point out that almost 80 percent of the wells are drilled by independents, not by major oil companies. There is competition out there. I am not afraid of bigness. I want to see that there is plenty of competition, and I believe that decontrol is the way this country ought to go.

The government is clearly and justifiably concerned about rip-offs and higher heating costs. The U.S. economy suffers from regional dislocations, and so we should talk about tax credits on home heating or wood burning or insulation. Some of this is in the administration's approach and some of it is not, but we need to be flexible, and to recognize that there are regional answers to some of the energy problems.

This is the program I think would work. I do think the government has a role, though I do not like the idea of its getting into fifty demonstration projects. If private industry is encouraged to invest in synthetics at costs that are not yet competitive with alternative sources, the government has a role, perhaps, in guaranteeing a market, or in guaranteeing some kind of loan, but I would rather see an indirect rather than a direct role for government.

I am asked about nuclear power. I believe this country should learn from Dr. Kemeny's report on the accident at Three Mile Island and we cannot turn our back on nuclear power. The president has a major job of educating the people and of inspiring confidence in this country. With his guidance, we should learn from that report and then go forward. Those who are opposed to nuclear power must explain how we will replace the energy—equivalent to 1.8 million barrels of oil a day—that comes from nuclear power in this country.

I believe the government has an important role in coordinating—with our allies, incidentally—the best research possible for commercial use of solar power. We need to do more things with our allies; this is an area that could excite the free world and offer hope to a lot of nonaligned countries.

The last point I would make on energy is that it is absolutely essential that we improve our relations with energy-producing countries. I have said over and over again that we must improve our relations with the moderate Arab countries and that we should understand Mexico better and improve relations with them. We cannot go down there as the big neighbor from the north and say, "Hey, you've got a lot of petroleum reserves, and here we are to help you take them out to fuel our excessive requirements in the United States."

I would like to make a comment critical of President Carter, which I hope will not be misunderstood. His comment about "Montezuma's revenge" in Mexico really offended the Mexicans. I have done business in Mexico. My daughter-in-law is a Mexican, and I could see in her eyes the hurt resulting from centuries of treating a proud people with less than full understanding of their problems, of their culture, of their pride. It was wrong for the President to say that, and it really hurt them. It reinforced their conviction of the way we look at them. We were wrong to turn down the gas deal with Mexico a year and a half ago and then to work it out under unsatisfactory conditions later on. We must turn that conviction around with a much more sensitive approach to foreign affairs.

In regard to relations with the moderate Arab countries, some people think we cannot keep our solemn commitment to Israel and at the same time improve relations with Israel's neighbors. I would like to discuss this, and I expect I will get a little challenge on it. I believe the Saudis are more concerned about our credibility vis-à-vis the Soviet Union than they are about the agreement between Egyptian President Anwar Sadat and Israeli Prime Minister Menachem Begin.

I know what the Arabs say. For two years at the United Nations I listened to what people said; then they would walk out the door and tell you what they mean. What they say and what they mean are sometimes two very different things. I believe that we can and must improve relations with the moderate Arab countries. I think it is in our interest to do it and that sound bilateral diplomacy can help do it.

That expresses my general view on energy. I favor decontrol, moving toward competitive market forces; in general, I believe that the President must do the maximum to ensure competition—not bigness, but competition. A continuing effort toward conservation is absolutely essential. The question of energy cannot be addressed without continually seeking new ways to improve on conservation, and that includes exploring new solutions with our foreign friends and allies. If we do these things, I think we can cope with this difficult problem.

My last point is what I call the window of danger. I look around this room and I feel a little inhibited in speaking about it, because some of the great experts in foreign policy are in this institute and in this room today. But I happen to believe that the United States is facing a dangerous period.

I am concerned about Soviet intentions. There was a debate in the intelligence community in the 1960s over whether the Soviets are driven by insecurity—an inferiority complex, by a desire to achieve parity—or by something more fundamental in their system that leads them to seek superiority.

I am convinced that they do not want war with the United States, or even confrontation now, but I believe that they seek not parity, but superiority. I also think there is a lot of evidence that they are doing things they should not be doing if they want real relaxation of tensions with the United States.

I believe we must turn around the U.S. perception that the Soviets are somehow softer or less aggressive than I think they are. We must do that, it seems to me, by first letting our allies know that we will keep our commitments. I am critical of President Carter for vacillating, pulling back. We started to vacillate on Korea. To a degree, Panama lends itself to the same objection. Iran clearly does. There was no simple answer in Iran, but I think we hastened the Shah's departure when we should have held back to look for some satisfactory answer.

When we look at Africa we see that we are up against an aggressive quest for hegemony on the part of the Soviet Union through its Cuban surrogate. I am unrelaxed about the recent disclosure of the combat brigade in Cuba, not because it represents a threat to those who want a vacation at the Fontainebleau, but because the Soviets are taking a step forward at a time the United States seems to be pulling back. When the President says the status quo is unacceptable and then accepts the status quo, it adds to the perception of a vacillating United States.

Our alliances should be strengthened.

We need to retune our human rights policy, not to retreat from our life-long national commitment to human rights, but so that we do not seem to be hypercritically selective in its application.

Strengthening rather than diminishing our intelligence capability fits in to a reversal of what I see as a retreat. This subject is near to my heart, since I was privileged to be director of the CIA for one year. People in the rest of the world wonder why the United States is willing to continue to see the authority of the CIA eroded. The CIA needs to be stronger; I am one, as some of you may remember, who helped draft an executive order and first implemented it to guarantee that the abuses of the past would not be repeated in the future. I further affirmed, in a very hostile environment, that we need a first-rate intelligence community for this country to remain free and to offer freedom to others. We have a good intelligence agency today, but it is not as good as it could be, because sources are simply unwilling to come forward if they think they will not be protected. Good intelligence is fundamental in assisting the president to make the right decisions on foreign affairs.

If we did those things—and there are plenty of other specific relationships we can talk about—I believe we would change this perception of the United States as pulling back and vacillating and being less than concerned.

We can also discuss some of the observations of the Carter administration on foreign affairs. I think Carter is claiming that the Caribbean is a victory for us in foreign policy. I am not quite sure what he meant when he said that he foresaw an era of peace and understanding there. My experience in foreign affairs makes me feel that having a pleasant relationship with the leader of some country or with an ambassador some place is not a yardstick for judging the effectiveness of foreign policy.

I hear that we have improved our relations with many nations in Africa, but how many times does the voting board at the United Nations light up with those nations siding with U.S. policy objectives? One cannot judge every amendment or every initiative at the United Nations chauvinistically, or always judge your friends by who is with you and who is against you. But you can judge trends. U.S. foreign policy has been based on human rights and continues to be based on human rights. We are a generous country, and we are a country that does not need to apologize, as we have been apologizing, for ourselves. I want to know which countries will be with us in the UN.

That does not mean that I am less interested in human rights than Jimmy Carter or Andy Young or anybody else. But I think I am calling for a more practical approach by which we try different policies, not just confrontational diplomacy, to seek change in human rights, an approach that recognizes that sometimes in our effort to affect instant change, we wake up and find that what follows cares less for human rights than what preceded.

That is a broad-brush description of the three most complicated problems that exist.

Let me end by saying that I am an idealist about this country. I am a total believer that we in the United States can solve any problem we want to solve. I know it will be tough and I know there will be a short period of great anxiety.

If we did instantly the things I suggested—and I am enough of a practical politician to know that would not happen—if we did these things instantly, there would still be some suffering, there would still be some hardship.

But I also know that some medicine will be necessary to get us out of this almost tragic period, into a much more sane economic period and a much more sound foreign policy period in the 1980s. We can do it. It will take leadership. It will take conviction. It will take, clearly, some shifts in the U.S. Congress.

The last point I want to make is this: People always talk about leadership today—and leadership is a key thing. Regardless of his conviction, his decency, one of the President's great shortcomings is what is perceived as his lack of leadership.

I think I have been able to lead and to do things on which the record would show that I have led. But leadership, for me, is not bullying allies, it is not dictating, it is not seeking confrontation; it is moving things forward and doing it with respect, preferably with the nation's integrity intact, putting forward the best side of our very sensitive system, and doing it with a certain constancy, a certain principle involved.

Nobody should be wed to every idea in the past as answers to the problems in the future. The person who is unwilling to make any change is a person who is too rigid truly to lead a country like this. But leadership has to be based on some principle. I have just touched the tip of the iceberg with what I think the principle should be. I feel confident that I could attract the kind of excellence that would help me lead this country. [Applause.]

DR. GOLDWIN: We are now ready for the audience to participate in the conversation.

ARAM BAKSHIAN, Washington writer: I wanted to explore a different area of the energy question. Since you have established that we need better understanding with the Islamic world, where do you go if you do not go as far as John Connally—or do you go as far as Mr. Connally? Essentially what is your policy toward the Islamic world vis-à-vis Israel, in particular?

MR. BUSH: I certainly do not go anywhere near John Connally on that question, because, frankly, I do not believe that the answer to the long-troubled area of the Middle East is the injection of permanent U.S. air power into the Middle East. I believe that that would draw the Soviet Union into a much more confrontational stance. It would be shortsighted for us to do that, and so I differ with Mr. Connally on that.

I do not want to put words into Mr. Connally's mouth, but the perception of trading an oil price for perhaps a lessened commitment to an ally goes against everything I have tried to spell out with regard to constancy in commitment. My argument with the Carter administration is that we do not appear to be willing to keep commitments. If we look as if we have gotten to the stage at which we have to trade off an ally, I think that is bad policy.

I am a little reluctant to discuss this with our expert Joe Sisco sitting here, but I have learned, sometimes with his help and with the help of others around this table, that the Middle East does not lend itself to a quick fix. It does not lend itself to an imposed settlement. One of the problems I had with the original Carter presentation was that it was going to be a comprehensive settlement. In my view, that, clearly, would have brought in the Soviet Union at Geneva when the Egyptians and the Sudanese and others have been trying to get them out.

If anyone had asked me two or three years ago, in my infinite wisdom, whether I would have predicted that the Begin-Sadat accords would have been possible, I probably would have said no, and I give the President credit for bringing Begin and Sadat together.

The peace process should be permitted to work with the United States as a catalyst, not as an imposer. I find nothing inconsistent in saying, in the same breath, that we should improve relations with the moderate Arab countries, or that we should be very concerned about the lack of humanity in Lebanon, or in other parts of the Arab world as well as in Israel.

The question then comes to talking with the Palestine Liberation Organization (PLO). Having looked at the covenant and conference of 1968 that labels Zionism an illegitimate force and Israel as the agent of Zionism, it does not require advanced logic to understand that is bad news for one of our allies. The PLO should recognize Israel's right to exist, and we should not talk to the PLO until it does.

We should push forward, however, recognizing that we must have good relations with the moderate Arab states. Some people will say this is impossible, but I simply do not believe it. I think King Hussein of Jordan eventually has a role in the peace plan, and I know that there is a role for him as a staunch ally of the United States.

But I cannot say precisely what ought to be done, because foreign policy decisions are part of an evolving process determined by what is happening right now.

I would be glad to be more specific on any parts I may have left out.

MR. BAKSHIAN: How would your Middle Eastern policy differ from the current policy?

MR. BUSH: I am not sure the administration is doing what I suggested with regard to the moderate Arabs, and I am not sure that we have left the impression with the Israelis that they can count on us as fully as they expect. My major thrust would simply be a shift in the way we handle our diplomacy. But I have no argument with just letting the peace process go forward with the Israelis and the Egyptians negotiating between themselves.

I have great difficulty with Israel establishing new settlements. There must be some constraint on the Israelis in making raids that kill civilians. But the other side of it is condoning or apparently acquiescing to terror as an acceptable force for political change in this world. We cannot do that. The PLO should renounce that; it should do the civilized, decent thing.

DAVID LICHTENSTEIN, Rockville, Maryland: George Will recently pointed out in a column that the Carter administration has posed the question of the Soviet brigade in Cuba in a very false context. The issue was presented as being very serious because it represented the potential for invasion of the United States, which is, obviously, ridiculous, and the administration therefore pointed out that the Soviet troops have no C-47s and cannot get to Florida.

Will points out, correctly, that the Soviet brigade is part of a worldwide logistics system that the Soviet Union has built up for transporting Cuban troops into Africa and other places.

My question is this: Would you be willing to use all the authority of the chief executive to prevent sales of wheat to the Soviet Union as a bargaining counter in handling this movement of Cuban troops into Angola, Mozambique, and so forth? How would you put a stop to this rapid expansion of Soviet power through the deployment of the Cuban guerrillas?

MR. BUSH: I am not sure I see this brigade as an integral logistical link with the 44,000 Cuban troops in Africa. I do know that when Gerald Ford left office, there were about 18,000 Cubans in Africa, and today there are 44,000. Some of that buildup occurred when we negated our

13

commitment to try to help the Savimbi forces in Angola. We made that decision on the false premise that we might get involved in another Vietnam. Yet I know of no backup plan that suggested that the United States was going to put troops into Angola. The Soviet Union was supporting one side and the United States was supporting what it thought was the non-Marxist side. That accounts for much of the Soviet presence in the continent of Africa.

Let me tell you what I would have tried to do on the Cuban problem. It is a serious matter and, incidentally, I do think it is wrong to set up a straw man about how this endangers Florida. That is not the issue. The issue is the acceptance of a Soviet force in that mode in this hemisphere for the first time, coincident with Castro's attempt to export his revolution again.

As you know, the Communists make a distinction between the support and the export of revolution. They may not have made a Politburo decision, but they have made some decision to export revolution to Central America. Indeed, they are drawing even closer to their close friends to the Caribbean.

I view that brigade as a symbol that we should not have accepted, and I agreed with President Carter that the status quo was unacceptable. I believe Carter thought he could hold out his hand with love to Cuba, but they bit that hand. I do not believe those troops were there before 1977.

What I would have tried to do is, before notifying Frank Church so he could look like a hawk in Idaho under fire—if you will excuse the political reference at this nonpolitical seminar—before doing that, I would have gotten hold of the Soviet Union quietly and said, "You have one hell of a problem. You want a lot from the United States." I would not necessarily have said grain, because I will always be thinking about what is the best for the United States.

But they need the Strategic Arms Limitation Treaty (SALT) more than we do. The constraints on their economy are very substantial— 40 percent more in real terms for arms in an economy that is less than half as big as ours. That is a pretty heavy economic burden, given some of the problems that the Soviet Union has today and some of the problems, such as energy, that it will have in the early 1980s. So, if we had said to them, "You've got a problem; now, before we go public, let's get the problem resolved, and figure out how you're going to satisfy the American people, who are going to be very concerned about this," I do not believe we would have lost all our leverage or all our bargaining power. And I would have laid it all out. That kind of diplomacy can still work. I believe that the Soviet Union really does not want a confrontation with the United States; it may some day, but not today. That is why I favor increases in defense spending.

But if that program did not work, I would have pushed forward as best I could, still with quiet diplomacy.

DR. GOLDWIN: Mr. Bush, I ought to clarify one thing I said before. Only AEI, as an institution, has to be concerned about being nonpartisan. You can be as partisan as you wish. [Laughter.]

MR. BUSH: Oh, I can? Okay. That's good. Now, let's get going here. [Laughter.]

WILLIAM FELLNER, American Enterprise Institute: I would like to ask a question that does not relate to foreign policy, but to taxes.

I think that indexation is not really a tax cut. Indexation is an avoidance of tax increases that are going on all the time, and this year will be quite steep. We should not really present it as a matter of tax cuts, we should present it as a matter of avoiding an increase in the tax burden of both individuals and corporations, relative to their incomes, as a result of inflationary factors getting into the taxable income; that is to say they pay higher taxes even if they have no higher real incomes.

MR. BUSH: I agree.

DR. FELLNER: Now, if indexation of taxes is to be done for both individuals and corporations, then it may be perhaps too expensive for one year, if a large increase in the deficit is to be avoided and if we are to have an increase in the defense budget, which I suppose we all favor. So it might be sensible to have a program that extends over more than a year, and that ends up thoroughly indexing the tax structure and doing away with this year-to-year increase in the tax burden. The increase is not recognized by the public at large as such because there are too many complicating factors, but it is clearly a tax increase, and its undoing would have absolutely nothing to do with what one really means by tax cuts.

But the indexation should be done in accordance with who is overtaxed by how much, and not in an arbitrary fashion that revamps the tax structure all the time, with the excuse that we are now, in the aggregate, undoing the increase of the past few years. This is what has been happening.

15

MR. BUSH: Thank you, sir. Let me comment. I was not so clear as I should have been. To be very candid with you, I do not like the concept of indexing. There is a certain "giving up" about indexing that troubles me.

The proposal I made was to index after the President puts forward a balanced budget for the fiscal year 1982. The program I spelled out would permit the President to cut that tax in the calendar year 1980 by $20 billion, leaving out the politics, with every side of it revised— supply side, investment side, depreciation schedules, and tax credits. We should then hold growth to the level I mentioned, adding the figure we have used for regulatory relief, present the budget as in balance by fiscal year 1982, and then index. Under this program, the Congress would have to vote for a higher tax, to go for an increase, when the budget gets out of balance.

That is the only way that indexing really has appealed to me, because I think there is a certain myth to it. It accepts this ghastly feeling that inflation is inevitable and we cannot do anything about it. In July I was in Israel where they index taxi fares and government benefits and salaries and whatever—I think there is a certain giving up about indexing, when it should instead be used rather selectively.

The last point I would make is this: I go around this country politically (now that we can talk politics here), and people tell me that President Carter says he cut taxes. Cut taxes? We are spending $46 billion more in taxes this year than last year. That is no tax cut. This situation is a little like gerbils running around inside an exercise wheel. I gave my grandson a gerbil for Christmas, and I watched it run like the devil, until it woke up, after about fifteen minutes, exhausted, and was right where it started.

The American people know something is being done to them, but they are not quite sure what it is. After the budget is in balance, indexing would let them know what it is, because those people who are talking one way and voting another would have to stand up and do their number.

DR. FELLNER: There is a very big difference, I think, between indexing wages and taxi fares on the one hand, and indexing the tax structure on the other. One really does something about the market process, where adjustments and overadjustments can take place, and the other is a legal commitment, about which the individual can do absolutely nothing. A nonindexed tax structure is simply a tax structure that, under inflationary circumstances, raises each income group's tax burden by a predictable margin, year after year. That is really something different from indexing and something that is subject to a market adjustment process.

Mr. Bush: May I make one frivolous addition to this weighty and learned conversation, at least weighty and learned on one side? [Laughter.]

I remember Bill Martin, chairman of the Federal Reserve, remarking in the late 1960s that a girls' school of which he was a trustee had voted to increase its tuition by $100 and then $200 a year. He felt that was a terrible commentary. I think the tuition rate then was $2,300 a year; at that same school the tuition is now something like $7,000 a year. I am not sure why it impressed me, but his point was that we are giving up on inflation.

When we start looking down the line, at an institution on one side or taxes on the other, we know the situation will become worse. One must be careful about not giving up, not suggesting that there is no other way for this country to go.

Dr. Fellner: That really is so.

Robert Nisbet, American Enterprise Institute: Mr. Bush, my question follows from your concluding remarks on the nature and responsibility of leadership, and I think I am addressing myself to your conception of the limits, or at least the moral limits, of the presidency in this country.

Even if there is no malaise—if that is an inappropriate word, or too strong—there is assuredly a perceptible waning of confidence in the minds of a great many Americans, and there is a very obvious retreat of a good many of the incentives—moral incentives, belief in progress, belief in work. Assuming that the condition I describe is actual—and I believe it is—we know from history that that is a very serious condition, indeed, in the life of any nation. My question comes to this: What do you see as the proper or legitimate role of the president with respect to the condition, the moral condition, that I have just described?

Mr. Bush: A very tough question. I believe that the post-Watergate morality should not be dead. Some people are saying that we have gone too far, and maybe we have, but I do not believe we should retreat from the concept of exemplary leadership at the top with regard to conflicts of interest, one's public behavior, or the effects of judgment as it affects a public life or career.

I have publicly laid on record my tax returns. My whole concept of the individual is that this disclosure is a real invasion of my privacy. I had Arthur Andersen, the accounting firm, prepare an audited statement far beyond the very vague legal requirement for FEC disclosure. I might say that Arthur Andersen was not overburdened by the assignment to prepare my net worth statement; nevertheless, I undertook it. I led the fight for disclosure in 1967 in Congress. One of our friends, who lost his seat in Congress in 1970, attributes some of his defeat to the fact that he went along with me on this concept of disclosure. His defeat stemmed from the fact that people in his state were not accustomed to their public officials having great wealth, and he had great wealth; but to his credit, he went along and made this full disclosure.

Disclosure, I think, is an invasion of one's personal privacy, but, transcending that, in the face of such cynicism about public service, it is a public good. That is a very small tip of the iceberg in response to a very, very tough question. But I just do not believe that leadership will be respected without that public morality.

MR. NISBET: I think what I failed to communicate is the distinction between the proper role of the president of the United States and the archbishop of a church.

To what extent is leadership manifest from the presidency of the United States when the president takes too direct a view of, or becomes too intimate with, matters of morality and spirit, instead of the hard problems of the economy, foreign policy, and defense?

MR. BUSH: Yes; moral pronouncement. This is a very delicate subject, because what I am about to say is something that I really have not been able to articulate.

I have great respect for President Carter in terms of his religious conviction. I have never questioned his sincerity, his decency, his relationship to his God, anything of that nature. I am not sure he has found what I think is the proper balance between his own religious convictions and leadership of this country. I do not think it is a proper role for the president of the United States to convert a Buddhist leader in another country. We have Buddhists in this country. Should they feel that they are less than good Americans?

We must be extraordinarily sensitive to the diversity of religions in this country, and there has been something that I have not been able to articulate that troubles me. I do not want to feel I am less religious because I do not share every detail or every item of our President's convictions on religion and morality. Objectivity in moral judgment is debatable and difficult. But we can come to some things that we would all agree are good or evil. My experience in life has taught me that the world does not lend itself to that kind of wishful simplicity, and leading this country calls for great sensitivity on the subject of diversity.

That may not get right to the heart of your question, but it would be the way I would conduct myself in this office.

JEANE KIRKPATRICK, American Enterprise Institute: I would like to raise a question about the Republican nomination contest, a political question.

MR. BUSH: I was hoping somebody would ask that question. I feel so good and so confident, watch me come alive now. Go ahead. [Laughter.]

DR. KIRKPATRICK: It is often said that Governor Reagan and Congressman Crane are conservatives in this race for the Republican nomination, that Howard Baker is a moderate, and that you are a moderate. People have more trouble with labels on John Connally. What I would like to know, if you can tell me, is whether you feel that these differences in labels reflect significant differences in policy positions in either domestic or foreign affairs.

MR. BUSH: No, I do not feel that they do. I do not like to be pinned down on labels. That is not because I have trouble knowing what I am, but because labels mean different things to different people. If a candidate goes to a black church in the fifth ward of Texas and calls himself a conservative, the people there will think he means to keep them in their place, or something racial.

When I say I am a conservative—I have absolutely no difficulty saying that—I am talking about what I think is economic sense. That should not be interpreted as a lack of sensitivity when it comes to social change or helping someone get a running start in the productive wage-earning period of his life or in his education.

I do not think there is a wide array of differences among the candidates. I was asked, very frankly, whether I agreed with John Connally on the Middle East. I do not, and I see nothing wrong with stating it, but I do not seek all kinds of differences to prove I am a moderate, a moderate-conservative, or whatever.

There is more of a matrix, more of a center, more of an agreement among the Republican candidates this year than in the past. I have had a consistent voting record on the kinds of economics we have talked about here today. My position on foreign affairs has been consistent. I am, however, recognizing that people can change on things. One must be able to change.

Consistency is equated only with conservatives, and I do not think that is particularly good. I do think a politician must adhere to a philosophical conviction, but I do not like labels, because somebody else interprets them differently.

I do not think there will be too wide a difference among Republican candidates on issues. I do not like these single issues that divide. In a partisan sense, the Republican candidates have a great opportunity to make a substantial change next time.

It is counterproductive to attempt always to fine-tune these labels. In the 1964 elections, there was a wide divergence between Barry Goldwater and Nelson Rockefeller. But I do not think there will be that wide a range among the candidates that emerge from these early primary and caucus states. I think they will be fairly close together, and the choice will boil down to a discussion of qualities such as leadership, experience, and diversity of background.

DALE TAFT, Kiplinger Washington Editors: What is your game plan for winning the Republican nomination against what I perceive to be rather formidable odds at this point?

MR. BUSH: You know, Mr. Taft, I used to get my feelings hurt, though I never let it show, when people would say, "George who?" The worst was when they would laugh and say, "President of what?"

I do have a relatively low name identification. I rather confidently feel I have had a breadth of experience that no other candidate has, and I am talking about a lifetime of service to my country. So what I have to do is get out there and get people to understand that.

My campaign staff and I set a game plan a year ago. The chief ingredients were to travel incessantly—a year ago it was to help other candidates—to make a final decision on running, and then to work harder, go more miles, travel, and get known by building organization. And what I am concentrating on is building organization in states with early primaries, and I believe the validation of that game plan is materializing.

There were three straw polls in Iowa last week. One of them was a dinner attended by every candidate other than Reagan. I won every vote by two to one, or two and one-half to one, over my closest rival, the last poll with 1,800 people. Now, those 1,800 people are activists; but remember, Iowa usually votes 30,000 to 40,000 people in the caucuses. If each one of those people brought in ten friends, that would be close to 50 percent of the vote. That is an oversimplification, but our plan is to organize in these early states and raise money. The mix of organization and advertising, the attention placed on this race, and the analysis of views of people and comparisons of candidates will make the difference.

The early states are states where I will do very, very well. I will not claw my way to this nomination by tearing down somebody else, I will put forward sensible proposals, I will resist the overpromise, and I believe there is evidence appearing that it can work.

We moved from a really discouraging 2 percent in the New Hampshire polls to 8 percent, but I am past one of the big guys in Iowa who has much higher name identification in the state of New Hampshire. I have Reagan's chairman from 1976 working for me; I have Ford's chairman from 1976 working for me, and we are building in these early states.

I know how to do it. I believe in our party. I have worked in the Republican party as a precinct chairman, a county chairman, and a national chairman. Although that is not so important in a general election, it is disproportionately important in the early stages of the political nominating process.

My campaign is coming together, and people are beginning to realize that George Bush cannot be written off. Polls are beginning to show a little movement. We will keep on with our game plan, and I believe it will work. I am absolutely confident of it today.

GEORGE WHITE, TV station WETA, Washington: Mr. Bush, I have a question that involves both leadership and the tyranny of labels, if you will. I think it is apparent that the executive cannot do much in the way of leadership without the support of the legislative branch. Would you care to comment on how the executive can achieve that support in this day and time?

MR. BUSH: First let me comment on pure politics. I think that we have witnessed the beginning of change in 1978. The Republicans picked up substantial numbers of seats in state legislatures. That was relatively unnoticed by people who are wrestling with the issues we are talking about today.

Proposition 13 surfaced. Republicans picked up seats in the Senate. We picked up a handful of seats, not nearly so many as I expected, in the House. We did well in the governorships. Great

Britain subsequently looked to me as if it moved away from European socialism. Canada sent the world a kind of answer.

I think there is a major trend out there, and I know there is a trend in this country when we hear Teddy Kennedy, whose voting record by any analysis is over with George McGovern or even further left, saying that the answers of the past do not glorify the future, or whatever that rhetoric is; something is going on, he is getting a message.

The kind of change we are talking about can be effected by a continuation of this trend that, in my view, started in 1978. The Republicans have a shot at control of the Senate, which may or may not work out, but there will also be a philosophical shift in the Congress.

I have a close friend who is a liberal Democrat. If he and I had both stayed home when I was in Congress, we would have saved the taxpayers, at that time, $75,000 a year (we were each being paid $37,500). We would have saved that amount because we cancelled each other out on almost every vote. After the 1976 election, I asked him what he was doing back in Congress; I thought that was the year we were going to knock off the liberals. He said, "You'd have been proud of me. I sounded just like Barry Goldwater."

Now, I do not know whether he is voting the way Barry Goldwater did, but his constituency, which is a labor constituency, sent him a message that it wanted something different.

I really believe that the answer to your question lies in political change. If that does not work, if a president is elected and the philosophical bent of Congress has not shifted enough to try programs such as I have outlined, another alternative is the veto.

We forget that that has been effective in the recent past. Let's give President Ford some credit. When he took office, inflation was 12 percent. There are many great economists here, and I do not want to get into business cycles and where we were on those cycles, but I believe part of the reason he had reduced inflation to 4.8 percent when he left office was that he vetoed legislation that would have blasted the spending side of his budget.

I feel there will be a shift in the country; it is moving toward these general principles that I think are Republican, others would say conservative. If I am elected on these principles, I would move quickly while there was still a mandate out there that people felt their congressmen should respond to.

Beyond that, it is extraordinarily difficult. Congress continues to pull away, further eroding the presidency. When the chairman of a

22

congressional subcommittee tries to shift the foreign policy of the United States on some issue or another, Congress has gone a long way in usurpation of presidential power. It can be gotten back, partly through leadership, partly through the makeup of the Congress itself. I would also want to consider whether legislation might be required.

MARY GALLAGHER, attorney, Washington, D.C.: You say that you would limit the increase in federal spending to 6.8 percent, Mr. Bush. There are a number of federal expenses that go up whether or not anyone proposes new federal spending; for example, government salaries. How could you do it?

MR. BUSH: I spoke of limiting the growth of spending to 6.8 percent a year. The Holt-Regula substitute, the budget amendment that would cut spending in fiscal year 1980, had a wide range of places that bring spending down, on a nickel and dime basis, on about thirty items. I do not have the list here, but it holds the growth in the later years of a wide range of social services, of counter-cyclical revenue, of the Comprehensive Employment Training Act (CETA)—I do not include defense spending, because encompassed in these numbers and in this formula that I have spelled out is an increase in defense spending. The numbers do come together.

Some of it, you're right, is uncontrollable. But some social welfare spending has grown disproportionately. While I do not think that Republicans, or those who agree with me on this, should be positioned as lacking compassion, I still feel that welfare spending should not grow as recklessly or as fast in the future as it has in the past.

I cannot give you the exact list, but it is there and it is documentable. We are not talking about major difficulties. I am saying, however, there are things that I would cut. I do not favor the Department of Education—let's be candid—because I think its creation will result in a tremendous growth in federal spending.

When former Health, Education, and Welfare Secretary Joseph Califano says there is $6 billion waste in HEW—let's go ferret out some of it and reduce that percentage of waste.

So I am not saying that priorities do not need to be reevaluated, but considering that growth has been around 7 to 9 percent, we will not be using a meat axe on programs that are helping people.

ROBERT WOODSON, American Enterprise Institute: Traditional wisdom in urban policy provides for tax incentives for large businesses to relocate in urban centers or to remain there as a source of employment. Our tax laws are geared toward businesses that are capital-intensive and high technology, when, in fact, research suggests that most of the new jobs are produced by small businesses; 90 percent, I believe, are plants that have ancillary buildings in small communities.

What is your position regarding this situation?

MR. BUSH: I do favor utilization of the tax system to encourage businesses to locate where there are concentrations of unemployed. I do favor private sector job training credits, for example. I think those are good things, and the evidence may be that that works better with small business, but this would be applicable to both large and small businesses, and I think that is a much better answer than training people for jobs that do not exist.

MR. WOODSON: But my point is that most of our tax incentives are for large businesses to relocate. We provide very little incentive for small businesses, even though the small businesses provide 90 percent of all new jobs.

MR. BUSH: I am not familiar with the numbers, but clearly that is something that ought to be changed. I agree that small business can be more readily responsive to some of these things. A very good point. I just did not know the numbers.

MICHAEL MALBIN, American Enterprise Institute: I would like to ask a follow-up question to two of the questions that were put previously. I notice that you were responding favorably to Mr. Nisbet's question on the issues of malaise and lack of work incentive, and so forth, but I was not satisfied that you answered fully on what you believe the role of presidential power is in trying to deal with issues that may manifest themselves primarily in attitudes of citizens.

Do you believe that it is the role of the president to address these issues directly? If so, how? Or do you believe that the only way or the best way for the president to deal with this is indirectly through forceful and competent handling of economic and other technical issues?

MR. BUSH: Help me with the clarification. What kind of issue are you talking about?

MR. MALBIN: Mr. Nisbet spoke of persistent malaise, lack of faith in progress, lack of belief in the work ethic.

MR. BUSH: I think there is definitely a responsibility to speak on some of those kinds of things. The president has a responsibility to speak out on kindness, and compassion, and that sort of thing. But I confess to being very careful in the religious area, in formalizing one's own denominational convictions and letting them spill over into governing. That gets very close to a violation of church and state separation, in my mind.

MR. MALBIN: Should the president, a person whose time is terribly limited, who could easily spend all of his time on economics or on defense issues, invest major portions of his time in simply giving speeches designed to set a moral tone?

MR. BUSH: No. The president should not talk like an evangelist but certainly should use the office to speak on things like the work ethic, the importance of family, the importance of keeping this country free so people can worship in their own way.

Historically, every president has done that. If the question is, how many hours a day should be allocated, it does not lend itself to that. The thrust ought to be running things, but people ought to look to the president as a person who can speak out on the fundamental values of our society, the values that have made us strong—neighborhood, family particularly—without going into all the specifics, leaving room for people to have diverse views on these things.

ALDO BECKMAN, *Chicago Tribune*: I would like to get to a specific issue that I think the president who is elected next November will have to face. You mentioned nuclear power as something we will have to learn to live with because we need it. Have you given any thought to what you will do with nuclear waste?

MR. BUSH: What I would do is say that we should get the best international technology to find an answer. There is an answer, solidification of waste. There is no short-run storage problem. There is an answer. Solidification in subterranean storage, safe subterranean storage areas. And a long-term answer can be found.

To say we cannot go forward because the final answer is not in our possession—I do not accept that limited and rather pessimistic view of U.S. technology.

WALTER BERNS, American Enterprise Institute: Mr. Bush, may I suggest something to add to your answer when next you are asked that question? About 98 percent of the waste that is now being generated is being generated in our own military atomic facilities. About 2 percent of the waste results from generating nuclear power. We will have the waste problem whether or not we produce nuclear power. You are right that we have to solve the waste problem. You are also right, as I understand it, that it is easily solvable.

DR. GOLDWIN: Thank you, Mr. Bush.
   [Applause.]